Great WFH Lunch Ideas

The Ultimate Guide to Awesome Lunch Recipes

By

Angel Burns

❤ ❤ ❤ ❤ ❤ ❤ ❤ ❤ ❤ ❤ ❤ ❤ ❤ ❤ ❤ ❤ ❤ ❤ ❤

License Notices

This book or parts thereof might not be reproduced in any format for personal or commercial use without the written permission of the author. Possession and distribution of this book by any means without said permission is prohibited by law.

All content is for entertainment purposes and the author accepts no responsibility for any damages, commercially or personally, caused by following the content.

Table of Contents

Introduction.. 7

Lunch Recipes.. 11

    Lunch Box Pizzas... 12

    Tasty Snack Ball... 14

    Tomato Sandwiches Lunch.. 16

    Lunch Sausages and Lentils.. 18

    Tuna Crunch Lunch.. 20

    Cottage Lunch Salad.. 22

    Luscious Lunch Wrap... 24

    Blueberry Protein Smoothie... 26

    Blueberry Almond Shake... 28

    Lemon Ricotta Blueberry Smoothie... 30

    Peanut Butter Blueberry Smoothie... 32

    Lime Raspberry Smoothie.. 34

    Delicious Raspberry Cheesecake Smoothie................................ 36

    Chicken Verde Casserole... 38

Chicken Mole 40

Adobo Marinated Chicken with Pickled Onions 44

Jalapeno Baked Chicken Thighs 47

Green Chile Chicken Tacos with Tomatillo Sauce 50

Seasoned Chicken Cheese Relleno 53

Chicken Enchiladas with Salsa Verde 56

Chicken Shrimp Paella 58

Cilantro Roasted Chicken Breasts 61

Instant Pot Chicken Carnitas 63

Chicken Street Tacos 66

Mexican Stewed Chicken with Capers 69

Everyday Beef Taco Meat Filling 72

Beef and Bean Enchiladas 74

Birria de Res (Mexican Beef Stew) 77

Slow Cooker Mexican Shredded Beef 80

Chili Colorado 82

Cheesy Chorizo Flautas 84

Sweet Pork Tacos 86

Chili Lamb Tacos 89

Fish Tacos 92

Veracruz Sea Bass 94

Mexican Ceviche 96

Seafood Enchiladas 98

Spicy Fish Taco Bowls 101

Spicy Shrimp Quesadillas 104

Shrimp a la Diabla 106

Refried Beans 108

Chili Rellenos 110

Mexican Rice 113

Quick and Easy Frijoles Charros 115

Poblanos with White Beans 117

Mexican Street Corn 119

Pepperoni Chaffle Pizza 121

Mini Keto Bacon Chaffle Pizza 123

Pizza Hut Style Chaffle Pizza 126

Japanese Style Chaffle Pizza 128

BBQ Chicken Chaffle Sandwich 130

Cinnamon Cream Cheese Chaffle 133

Mozzarella Peanut Butter Chaffle 135

Conclusion 137

About the Author 138

Author's Afterthoughts 139

Introduction

Optimizing Your Health and Wellbeing

Working from home creates other challenges too. Chief among these is trying to look after yourself and your wellbeing.

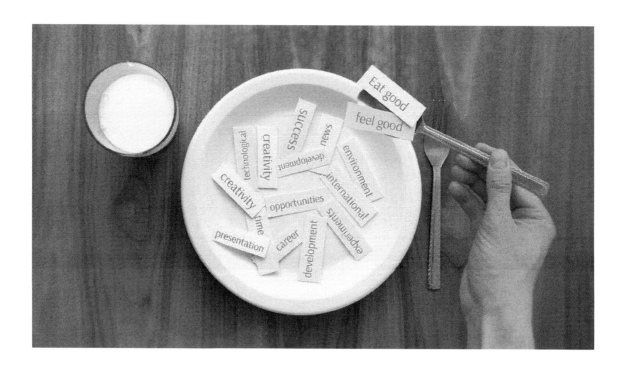

When you don't leave the house to go to work, there is no incentive to dress well. When no one sees you for days, there is no requirement to wash.

And when you can get up at any time you want, and work at any time you like, there is nothing stopping you from losing all semblance of routine and health.

What's more, is that because you don't need to go to work, there is no guarantee that you'll get any fresh air or exercise! These are all serious issues because they can be detrimental to your health and wellbeing.

Indeed, when work gets on top of you, you might even find yourself eating poorly as you grab whatever is quick and stuff it in a microwave.

All this leads to your being tired, de-motivated, and less able to focus. Focusing and staying motivated requires energy, and resisting temptations and distractions likewise require that you are in good health.

- In short, if you don't look after yourself outside of work, you'll struggle to stay focused when you sit down at the computer.

Optimizing your health will allow you to focus better, seeing as focus requires energy. Using a disciplined routine will ensure you get proper time to rest and recover. And taking the time to groom yourself and look your best will help you to feel (and thus become) more productive and professional.

Getting Proper Downtime and Rest

Indeed, one of the most important things you can do to optimize yourself for productivity and output is to make sure that you get proper downtime and rest. Think of this as the "yin to the yang" of productivity.

What many people don't realize is that their effort and their focus are based on energy. And that their energy is a finite resource.

When you work from home, you might feel tempted to work longer hours in order to get more done. Because your office is in the same house, you can very easily put in an extra hour in order to better satisfy the client/earn more money/make tomorrow less stressful.

But guess what? If you do that, then you'll start tomorrow more tired, and you'll be less likely to get work finished.

We have a tendency to think that working late will help us to get more done, but studies show us that the work done at this time is lower quality AND that it tends to be far less pressing than we imagine.

This is why it's SO important that you make a clear distinction between "work time" and "downtime." Only by resting properly – which also means forgetting about the stressful aspects of your job – can you then come back to work the next day feeling restored and productive.

This means you should stop work at 5 pm (or whatever you have designated as the end of your day) EVEN if there is still work left to do.

AND it means that you should stop looking at your work emails. Many apps like Slack will allow you to turn off notifications outside of office hours. But you can also do this by owning two phones – one for work and one for getting things done.

It's also significant that you enjoy yourself during your downtime with things you like doing. That means reading books, playing games, chatting with friends, or watching movies.

One of the reasons we feel distracted at work is that our brain wants stimulation and entertainment. If you don't have any set time where you get to enjoy those things planned, then you will find it hard to turn off and focus on work during work hours. You need to "get it out of your system," so to speak!

If you stay positive and apply yourself consistently towards working from home effectively, then the results will come. Plan for your lunchtime meals.

Lunch Recipes

While working from home, it is certainly essential to ensure that you do not miss your lunchtime meal. Always find time to attend to your hunger needs and ensure you stay healthy. Here, we have simple meals for you to prepare and enjoy at home.

Lunch Box Pizzas

Pizzas are a wonderful way to enjoy your lunch. Lunch box pizzas will give you and your family the best, especially on a busy lunchtime.

Servings: 4

Cooking time: 20 minutes

Ingredients:

- ¼ c. tomato sauce
- 7 ½ oz. buttermilk biscuits, refrigerated
- 10 slices pepperoni
- 1 tsp. Italian seasoning
- ¾ c. Monterey jack cheese, shredded

Instructions:

1. Flatten every biscuit to form a 3-in. circle. Set into a muffin cup greased with cooking spray.

2. Mix together the Italian seasoning and tomato sauce. In each cup, set in approximately 1 teaspoonful of the mixture. Top with a slice of pepperoni and for approximately 1 tablespoon cheese.

3. Bake for about 15 minutes at 425°F. serve at once.

Tasty Snack Ball

The tasty snack ball is a quite yummy and delicious meal. A try of the meal, especially during lunchtime, will give you a perfect experience.

Servings: 3

Cooking time: 20 minutes

Ingredients:

- ½ c. flour
- ½ c. maple syrup
- ½ c. peanut butter
- ½ c. sunflower seeds
- ½ c. wheat germ
- ½ c. cocoa powder

Instructions:

1. Combine all ingredients using a bowl.

2. Roll into a small sphere

Tomato Sandwiches Lunch

Having a tomato sandwich for lunch is quite healthy for your body. These sandwiches are prepared in a wonderful way that will give you the best. Enjoy.

Servings: 3

Cooking time: 25 minutes

Ingredients:

- 4 fresh tomatoes, sliced
- 1 sliced white onion
- 1 tbsp. softened butter
- 8 slices fresh white bread
- 1 tsp. fresh chives

Instructions:

1. Combine onions, tomatoes, and chives

2. Spread butter on 4 slices of bread. Top the slices with the tomato mixture. Top with the remaining 4 slices. Lightly but firmly press the top bread onto tomato topped bread slices

3. Serve immediately with fresh iced tea beverage made from lemon juice and sugar

Lunch Sausages and Lentils

Craving for a delicious and mouth-watering lunchtime meal? Try the lunch sausages and lentils, and you will enjoy it.

Servings: 4

Cooking time: 40 minutes

Ingredients:

- 150 ml red wine
- Pepper
- 1 tbsp. sunflower oil
- 4 peeled and chopped onions
- 8 slices streaky smoked bacon
- 8 sausages
- Salt
- Fresh thyme
- 200g dry green lentils
- 4 chopped and peeled garlic cloves
- 300 ml good quality beef stock

Instructions:

1. Set onions in a pan and heat to soften.

2. Set in sausages, lentils, and garlic and stir. Cook for 1 minute.

3. Add oil in a dish and set to the oven. Add in the bacon and cook on medium until crispy. Set aside.

4. Prepare the sausages to brown them on both sides. Set aside and add stock butter and dry wine, then lower the heat to a slow simmer.

5. Simmer for 35 minutes until the sausages are well cooked.

6. Season accordingly and crumble in the bacon before serving.

7. Enjoy.

Tuna Crunch Lunch

Tuna Crunch Lunch is a perfectly wonderful idea to consider for a lunch meal. This meal entails essential ingredients that are wonderful for your health. Enjoy.

Servings: 4

Cooking time: 15 minutes

Ingredients:

- 4 whole wheat buns, sliced halfway
- 14 oz. drained tuna
- 3 tbsp. chopped celery
- 3 tbsp. chopped green onions
- Salt & pepper
- 1 c. grated cheddar cheese

Instructions:

1. Using a bowl, mix the first 4 ingredients.

2. Apply the pepper and salt for seasoning. Top with cheese and set in your oven to bake for about 15 minutes at 375°F.

Cottage Lunch Salad

It is a tasty and easy lunch you can ever hope for. The meal is made of unique and essential ingredients that will be loved by most of your family members.

Servings: 3

Cooking time: 20 minutes

Ingredients:

- 6 lettuce leaves
- 1 c. fat-free cottage cheese
- 2 chopped spring onions
- 1 stalk celery, chopped
- 1 chopped red radish
- ½ tsp. dried dill
- Salt & ground black pepper
- 1 sliced plum tomato
- 1 sliced red radish
- 10 sliced peeled cucumbers

Instructions:

1. In a bowl, add cheese, spring onions, chopped radish, celery, dill, pepper and salt, and mix.

2. Set 3 large lettuce leaves on each of two plates. Add the above mixture. Top with sliced radish, cucumber and tomatoes. Add more salt if desired.

Luscious Lunch Wrap

The Luscious Lunch wrap entails a combination of ingredients that are quite essential to your health. Enjoy.

Servings: 3

Cooking time: 15 minutes

Ingredients:

- 2 tbsp. mayonnaise
- Cheese slice
- Ham
- 2 flour tortillas
- Iceberg lettuce

Instructions:

1. Set the ham and combine together with other ingredients. Spread the cheese and add pepper and onions.

2. Top with tomato and wrap tightly before securing with a toothpick. Enjoy.

Blueberry Protein Smoothie

It is a wonderful boost to the health of your body. A try of the smoothie can also be absolutely amazing as you will be able to enjoy the sweetness that comes with it.

Servings: 2

Cooking time: 5 minutes

Ingredients:

- 2 tbsp. protein powder
- 1 tsp. stevia
- 2/3 c. blueberries
- ¾ c. almond milk, unsweetened

Instructions:

1. First, add all ingredients into the blender and blend until smooth.

2. Serve immediately and enjoy.

Blueberry Almond Shake

It's a perfect and delicious food you can ever think of for lunch. Try it and boost your health status.

Servings: 1

Cooking time: 5 minutes

Ingredients:

- 1 tbsp. almond butter
- ¼ c. blueberries
- 1 c. almond milk, unsweetened

Instructions:

1. First, add all ingredients into the blender and blend until smooth.

2. Serve immediately and enjoy.

Lemon Ricotta Blueberry Smoothie

It is a great way to continue with your day. A taste of Lemon Ricotta Blueberry smoothie will keep you craving for it.

Servings: 2

Cooking time: 5 minutes

Ingredients:

- 1/8 tsp. lemon zest
- ½ tsp. lemon juice
- 1 tsp. chia seeds
- ¼ c. almond milk, unsweetened
- ¼ c. ricotta cheese
- 1 c. blueberries

Instructions:

1. First, add all ingredients into the blender and blend until smooth.

2. Serve immediately and enjoy.

Peanut Butter Blueberry Smoothie

It will exactly make a wonderful and considerable lunch. You will actually enjoy it.

Servings: 1

Cooking time: 5 minutes

Ingredients:

- ¼ c. frozen blueberries
- 1 tbsp. peanut butter
- ½ c. heavy whipping cream
- ½ c. almond milk, unsweetened

Instructions:

1. First, add all ingredients into the blender and blend until smooth.

2. Serve immediately and enjoy.

Lime Raspberry Smoothie

The smoothie is a combination of the most favorite flavors. Enjoy the flavors that come from each and every ingredient.

Servings: 2

Cooking time: 5 minutes

Ingredients:

- 1 c. almond milk, unsweetened
- ¼ c. yogurt
- 2/3 fresh lime juice
- 1 c. raspberries

Instructions:

1. First, add all ingredients into the blender and blend until smooth and creamy.

2. Serve immediately and enjoy.

Delicious Raspberry Cheesecake Smoothie

It's a perfectly easy and delicious food that will give you all the sweetness. Enjoy the smoothie with friends and family.

Servings: 2

Cooking time: 5 minutes

Ingredients:

- 2 c. ice cubes
- 1 ½ tsp. vanilla extract
- ¼ tsp. liquid stevia
- 10 oz. raspberries
- ½ c. cottage cheese
- 1 c. coconut water

Instructions:

1. First, add all ingredients into the blender and blend until smooth and creamy.

2. Serve immediately and enjoy.

Chicken Verde Casserole

The meal is easily baked and everybody will love it. Enjoy it

Servings: 5

Cooking time: 25 minutes

Ingredients:

- 3 c. baked tortilla chips
- ½ c. chopped cilantro
- 8 oz. salsa verde
- 1½ c. frozen corn kernels
- 1 c. shredded Monterey jack cheese
- 1½ lb. halved bone-in chicken breasts
- Chopped Cilantro

Instructions:

1. Preheat your oven to 375°F.

2. Add half of the baked tortilla chips to a large baking dish.

3. Top the chips with half of the salsa verde, chicken breast halves, corn and shredded cheese.

4. Repeat these layers.

5. Cover with aluminum foil.

6. Bake for 20 minutes.

7. Remove the foil, then bake for 5 more minutes.

8. Remove and top with a garnish of chopped cilantro.

9. Serve warm

Chicken Mole

It is a classic meal that will be loved by many. With a range of ingredients, you will enjoy the flavors that come with it.

Servings: 8

Cooking time: 45 minutes

Ingredients:

- 3 tbsp. divided olive or peanut oil
- 1 ½ lb. boneless chicken breasts and thighs, skinless cut in pieces
- ½ tsp. ancho chile powder
- ½ tsp. salt
- 1 tsp. ground black pepper
- 1 ½ c. chicken stock
- 1 c. fresh orange juice
- 1 c. sliced yellow onions
- 4 cloves garlic, chopped
- 1 tbsp. sesame seeds
- ¼ c. sliced almonds
- 2 tsp. cumin seeds
- 2 tsp. coriander
- 1 tsp. crushed red pepper flakes
- 2 tsp. orange zest
- ¼ c. chopped ancho chiles
- 1 tbsp. chopped pasilla negro chiles
- 2 tbsp. chopped currants
- ½ c. chopped dark or Mexican chocolate
- Mexican Rice
- Fresh Cilantro or Parsley

Instructions:

1. First, heat half of the oil in your large, deep skillet over medium-high heat.

2. Season the chicken with the ancho chile powder, salt and black pepper.

3. Place the chicken in the skillet, then brown until lightly golden, approximately 3-4 minutes per side.

4. Add in the chicken stock and orange juice. Bring the liquid to a low boil. Reduce the heat to medium-low, cover and let simmer for 30 minutes, or until chicken is cooked through and actually no longer pink in the middle.

5. Meanwhile, after the chicken is about halfway through the cooking time, add the remaining oil to a large saucepan or deep sauté pan and heat over medium.

6. Add the onions and sauté for approximately 2-3 minutes.

7. Add the garlic, sesame seeds, and almonds. Cook for 2 minutes, toasting the seeds and the almonds lightly.

8. Season with cumin, coriander, orange zest and crushed red pepper flakes and cook until highly fragrant, approximately 3 minutes.

9. Add the chopped ancho chiles and pasilla negro chiles. Cook, constantly stirring until the chiles are tender, approximately 3-5 minutes.

10. Remove the cooked chicken from the pan and set aside.

11. Add the chicken broth from the chicken pan into the saucepan along with the currants. Mix well.

12. Cover, then let simmer for approximately 25 minutes.

13. While the sauce is simmering, either shred the chicken or cut it into bite-sized pieces and set aside.

14. Remove the sauce from heat, uncover and add the dark or Mexican chocolate. Mix well and let cool for 10 minutes.

15. Next, transfer the sauce to a blender or food processor and puree until smooth. You can either leave the sauce as is or run it through a fine-mesh sieve for a thinner consistency.

16. Add the sauce back into the skillet, along with the chicken and cook over medium-low heat until the sauce and the chicken are warmed through.

17. Serve with Mexican rice, garnished with cilantro or parsley.

Adobo Marinated Chicken with Pickled Onions

The meal is definitely part of the best meals to enjoy. Try it for lunch.

Servings: 4

Cooking time: 20 min.

Ingredients:

- 1 lb. sliced boneless chicken breast, skinless
- ¼ c. chopped chipotle peppers with adobo sauce
- 2 crushed cloves garlic, minced
- ¼ c. orange juice
- ¼ c. lime juice
- 1 tsp. orange zest
- 2 tbsp. olive oil
- 2 c. red onions, sliced
- 1 diced jalapeño pepper
- ¼ c. lime juice
- 2 tsp. white vinegar
- 1 tsp. white sugar
- ¼ c. chopped cilantro

Instructions:

1. In a bowl, combine the chipotle peppers with adobo sauce, garlic, orange juice, lime juice, orange zest, and olive oil. Mix well.

2. Add the chicken to the bowl, then cover with the marinade. Cover and refrigerate for at least 30 minutes.

3. In another bowl combine the red onions and jalapeño pepper. Toss to mix.

4. Combine the lime juice, white vinegar, white sugar, and cilantro. Mix well and pour over the onions. Cover, then set aside or refrigerate until ready to use.

5. Heat a skillet over medium heat.

6. Next, remove the chicken from the marinade, then place in the skillet. Cook, adding more olive oil if necessary, until the chicken is cooked through.

7. Remove the chicken and pour any remaining marinade into the pan.

8. Cook the remaining marinade over medium-high heat, stirring as it reduces slightly for 5-7 minutes. Add the chicken back into the skillet. Toss to coat before transferring to serving plates.

9. Serve garnished with the pickled onions.

Jalapeno Baked Chicken Thighs

It's a perfect and wonderful weekday meal that is a choice of many. Enjoy.

Servings: 8

Cooking time: 50 minutes

Ingredients:

- 1 tbsp. seasoned salt
- 1 c. all-purpose flour
- 1 tsp. pepper
- 1 tsp. salt
- 8 bone-in chicken thighs, skin removed
- ¾ c. milk
- 3 tbsp. olive oil
- 2 seeded jalapeno peppers, chopped
- 1 chopped onion
- 15 oz. tomato sauce
- 1 tbsp. chili powder
- 1 c. water
- 2 tsp. ground cumin
- 2 tsp. garlic powder
- Cooking oil

Instructions:

1. Preheat oven to 350°F (176°C).

2. In a medium-to-large bowl, mix the seasoned salt, flour, salt and pepper.

3. Place the milk in another bowl. Then, coat the chicken pieces with the flour mix, then put them in the milk and coat well again.

4. Brown the coated chicken in a large saucepan or skillet with the oil and then transfer it to a baking dish.

5. Into the same skillet, add the jalapenos and onions. Cook until they turn translucent.

6. Mix in the water, tomato sauce and spices and bring to a boil.

7. Reduce heat, then simmer for 5 minutes until thickened.

8. Add the mixture over the browned chicken pieces.

9. Cover the baking dish and bake for 30–35 minutes.

10. Serve warm.

Green Chile Chicken Tacos with Tomatillo Sauce

The most satisfying meal that can be tried on a busy lunch is the Green Chile Chicken Tacos with Tomato Sauce. Try the meal and enjoy the best.

Servings: 4

Cooking time: 20 minutes

Ingredients:

- 1 lb. cooked chicken, shredded
- 1 tsp. divided salt
- 1 tsp. white pepper
- 1 tsp. Mexican oregano
- 4 tbsp. butter, divided
- 2 arbol chilies, or other dried chile
- 1 c. hot water
- 2 c. tomatillos, quartered
- 1 c. poblano pepper, sliced
- 1 tsp. seeded jalapeño pepper, diced
- 4 crushed divided cloves garlic, minced
- ¼ c. freshly chopped cilantro
- Fresh corn tortillas

Instructions:

1. Season the chicken with one half of the salt, white pepper, and Mexican oregano.

2. Heat 1 tablespoon of butter in a skillet on the stove top over medium heat.

3. Add the arbol chilies and sauté until fragrant, approximately 2-3 minutes. Remove the chilies from the pan, then place in a bowl covered with hot water. Let sit for 5-10 minutes.

4. Add the tomatillos and 2 cloves of garlic to the skillet. Sauté until browned and tender, approximately 5-7 minutes.

5. Chop up the hydrated chilies and place them in a blender along with the tomatillos mixture, remaining butter from the pan and cilantro. Puree until smooth.

6. Next, place your skillet back on the heat and melt 1 tablespoon of butter. Add the chicken and cook for 5-7 minutes, until browned and heated through. Remove the chicken from the skillet, then set aside.

7. Add the poblano pepper, jalapeño pepper, and remaining garlic to the skillet and sauté for 2-3 minutes. Stir in the chicken.

8. Serve the chicken and peppers in fresh tortillas, garnished with the tomatillo sauce.

Seasoned Chicken Cheese Relleno

The meal is not quite spicy, but the sweetness that comes with it is amazing. Enjoy

Servings: 6

Cooking time: 30 minutes

Ingredients:

- 2 tbsp. taco seasoning mix
- 4 oz. whole green chilies
- 1 beaten egg
- ⅓ c. cornmeal
- 6 boneless and skinless chicken breasts, sliced
- 2 oz. Monterey Jack cheese, cut into 6 strips
- 2 oz. Monterey Jack cheese, shredded
- 8 oz. red taco sauce
- ¼ tsp. crushed red pepper
- 2 tbsp. chopped cilantro

Instructions:

1. Preheat oven to 375°F (190°C).

2. Mix the taco seasoning mix and cornmeal in a medium-to-large bowl. Beat the egg in another bowl.

3. Slit the chilies lengthwise and slice into thin pieces.

4. Arrange the chicken breasts; top them equally with half a chili slice, a piece of cheese, and some cilantro and crushed red peppers. Roll them up.

5. Next, dip each chicken roll in egg, and then cornmeal; arrange in a shallow baking dish.

6. Bake uncovered for 30 minutes.

7. Pour the taco sauce over the chicken and sprinkle cheese on top.

8. Serve warm.

Chicken Enchiladas with Salsa Verde

It is a quicker version that will be enjoyed most. Have a taste of it and enjoy

Servings: 2

Cooking time: 5 minutes

Ingredients:

- 1 c. shredded ricotta cheese
- 1 c. lettuce, finely chopped
- 4 corn tortillas
- 2 c. shredded roasted chicken, cooked
- 1 chopped onion

- 2 c. green salsa
- Salt and pepper

Instructions:

1. Mix the cheese, chicken, lettuce, onion, salt and pepper in a medium-to-large bowl.

2. Heat the green salsa in a saucepan over medium-low heat; add the tortillas. Mix well and place them on a plate.

3. Top ¼ of the prepared mixture over each tortilla and fold to make rolls.

4. If you want, pour the extra green salsa over the rolls.

5. Serve warm.

Chicken Shrimp Paella

Enjoy the sweetness that comes with the delicious chicken shrimp paella.

Servings: 4

Cooking time: 40 minutes

Ingredients:

- 1 tsp. turmeric powder
- ¼ lb. sliced boneless chicken breast
- 1 chopped onion
- Juice of 1 lemon
- Handful of parsley leaves
- ¼ lb. shrimp
- 2 c. rinsed rice
- 1-quart chicken broth
- 1 c. chorizo
- Salt
- 1 c. green peas
- 1 chopped small red bell pepper
- 2 tsp. freshly grated garlic
- ¼ c. butter
- 1 tsp. paprika
- Pepper

Instructions:

1. First, in a saucepan over medium-high heat, melt the butter.

2. Add onion and stir until it is translucent.

3. Add garlic to cook for a minute.

4. Add shrimp, chicken, bell pepper, green peas, turmeric powder and seasonings.

5. Cook the shrimp to softness and until it turns light pink.

6. Add paprika, parsley, broth and rice.

7. Mix well before covering the pan with a tight lid.

8. Let the mixture simmer on low heat until the chicken is cooked through.

9. Serve warm and enjoy.

Cilantro Roasted Chicken Breasts

It is a perfect weekday meal. Prepare it and enjoy with family.

Servings: 4

Cooking time: 20 minutes

Ingredients:

- 1 tbsp. olive oil
- 1 c. shredded Oaxaca cheese
- 1 lb. skinless, boneless chicken breast
- 1 tsp. Mexican oregano
- 1 tsp. garlic powder
- 1 tsp. black pepper
- 1 c. sliced yellow onions
- 1 tsp. salt
- ½ c. chopped fresh cilantro
- 2 quartered ears fresh corn
- 1 c. salsa verde

Instructions:

1. Preheat the oven to about 3750F.

2. Next, rub the chicken breast with olive oil and add seasonings, garlic powder and Mexican oregano.

3. In a baking tray, combine the chicken with onions and corn.

4. Combine salsa verde and cilantro then mix well and pour over the chicken.

5. Add Oaxaca cheese topping and put into an oven.

6. Bake for about 20 minutes until the chicken is cooked through.

7. Serve and enjoy.

Instant Pot Chicken Carnitas

Enjoy the taste of a traditional Mexican dish.

Servings: 6

Cooking time: 30 minutes

Ingredients:

- 2 seeded and chopped Serrano peppers
- 1 tbsp. dried oregano
- 2 lb. skinless, boneless chicken breasts
- 2 tbsp. kosher salt
- 2 tsp. cumin
- 1 coarsely chopped white onion
- 4 minced garlic cloves
- 1 quartered orange
- 1 tbsp. olive oil
- Water
- Cooking spray
- 2 tsp. cracked pepper

Instructions:

1. Brush olive oil on the chicken breasts and season with cumin, pepper, oregano and salt.

2. Transfer the chicken into an instant pot and garlic, peppers and onion.

3. From the orange, squirt the juice over the top and put the orange into the Instant pot.

4. Close the lid to cook for 20 minutes on high pressure.

5. Do a natural pressure release for 10 minutes and manually release the remaining pressure.

6. Put the chicken into the broiler and broil for 10 minutes until crispy.

7. Serve with tortillas and toppings of your choice.

8. Enjoy.

Chicken Street Tacos

It is a common food that is great and wonderful. Enjoy the Chicken Street Tacos.

Servings: 4

Cooking time: 10 minutes

Ingredients:

Hot sauce

- 22 warmed mini white corn tortillas
- ½ c. chopped fresh cilantro
- Fresh lime juice
- 1½ lb. boneless skinless chicken thighs
- Sour cream
- Pico de gallo

For the marinade:

- 2 tsp. dried oregano leaves
- 1 tsp. salt
- 2 tsp. paprika
- ¼ tsp. ground cinnamon
- 4 tbsp. orange juice
- 1½ tbsp. lime juice
- Freshly ground black pepper
- 3 minced garlic cloves
- 1½ tbsp. chipotle chili powder
- 2 tbsp. apple cider vinegar

Instructions:

1. First, in a large plastic bag, combine all the ingredients for the marinade.

2. Add chicken thighs and marinate for about 30 minutes.

3. Shred the chicken and serve with tortillas, fresh lime juice, cilantro and any other desirable topping.

Mexican Stewed Chicken with Capers

The recipe is authentic and heat-warming. You will enjoy the appetizing taste. Enjoy it.

Servings: 6

Cooking time: 45 minutes

Ingredients:

- 2 c. chicken stock
- ¼ c. capers
- 1 tsp. salt
- 1 ½ lb. bone-in chicken pieces
- ¼ tsp. ground cloves
- 1 c. sliced white onion
- ½ tsp. cinnamon
- ½ c. sliced poblano pepper
- 2 crushed and minced garlic cloves
- 1 tsp. black pepper
- 4 c. crushed roasted tomatoes with liquid
- 2 tbsp. olive oil

Instructions:

1. In a large cast skillet over medium heat, heat the olive oil.

2. To the chicken, add salt and pepper accordingly and put it to the skillet until both sides are golden brown. Set the chicken aside.

3. Add crushed tomatoes with liquid, garlic, pablano pepper and onion to the skillet. Cover to cook for about 5 minutes. Uncover and cook for 5 more minutes as the sauce starts to reduce.

4. Add capers and chicken stock then season with cinnamon and cloves. Then, adjust the heat to bring the sauce to a low boil.

5. Transfer the chicken back into the skillet and lower the heat to medium and cook for 30 more minutes until the chicken is well cooked.

6. Serve and enjoy.

Everyday Beef Taco Meat Filling

Enjoy the sweetness that comes with this simply prepared dish.

Servings: 4

Cooking time: 12 minutes

Ingredients:

- ½ tsp. minced onion
- ½ c. water
- 1 tbsp. chili powder
- ⅛ tsp. garlic powder
- ⅛ tsp. cumin
- ½ tsp. paprika
- 1 tsp. salt
- ¼ tsp. onion powder
- 1 lb. ground beef

Instructions:

1. Mix paprika, onion, chili powder, salt, cumin, garlic powder, onion powder and beef in a medium mixing bowl.

2. Add beef mixture to cook for 12 minutes with occasional stirring

3. Spoon the mixture into tacos and add a favorite topping.

4. Serve and enjoy.

Beef and Bean Enchiladas

The dish is super easy and delicious to enjoy with friends and family.

Servings: 6

Cooking time: 25 minutes

Ingredients:

- 10 oz. enchilada sauce
- 15 oz. rinsed and drained black beans
- 10 corn tortillas
- Green onions
- Chopped cilantro
- 1 diced yellow onion
- 2 tbsp. olive oil
- 3 c. Mexican blend shredded cheese
- 2 garlic cloves
- Salt
- 1½ lb. ground beef
- 4 oz. green chilies
- Pepper

Instructions:

1. Preheat the oven to about 1760C.

2. Next, in your medium saucepan over medium heat, heat the oil

3. Add ground beef then brown evenly

4. Add green chilies, onion and garlic then sauté for 5 minutes.

5. Set the tortillas on a plate and evenly top with enchilada sauce over it. Add some beans topping.

6. Add the beef mixture, additional sauce and some cheese topping.

7. Roll it and put in a well-greased baking pan.

8. Do the same for the remaining tortillas and reserve some sauce.

9. Bake for 20 minutes uncovered and until the cheese is golden brown.

10. Add chopped cilantro and green onion topping.

11. Serve and enjoy.

Birria de Res (Mexican Beef Stew)

It is a perfect stew that one can give a try. Enjoy.

Servings: 6

Cooking time: 6 hours 30 minutes

Ingredients:

- 5 dried Guajillo chilies
- Salt
- 2 garlic cloves
- 1 tsp. dried oregano
- 2 bay leaves
- 1 tsp. dried thyme
- 1 clove
- ¼ cinnamon stick
- 4 c. water
- 1 tbsp. beef bouillon
- 4 lb. roast beef
- 2 dried deseeded and deveined Ancho chilies
- 2 tbsp. oil
- Pepper

Instructions:

1. In a skillet over high heat, add chilies to cook for one minute on each side.

2. Transfer the chilies to a medium bowl and add a cup of hot water to soak for about 5 minutes. Reserve the water.

3. To the same skillet, add oil and then add the roast to the pan to brown each side.

4. In a blender, add the reserved water along with seasonings, laurel leaves, bouillon, beef, clove, thyme and oregano and puree until the sauce is smooth.

5. To the slow cooker, add the browned roast and top with chili sauce to cook for 8 hours on low heat. Shred the beef, then keep it in the sauce.

6. Serve with a topping of your choice and enjoy.

Slow Cooker Mexican Shredded Beef

Enjoy the sweetness that underlies each and every ingredient.

Servings: 6

Cooking time: 8 hours

Ingredients:

- 1½ tsp. cumin
- 1 tsp. onion powder
- 1½ tsp. chili powder
- 3 lb. beef chuck shoulder roast
- Pepper
- 2 c. beef broth
- 15-oz. stewed tomatoes
- ½ tsp. chipotle chili powder
- 1 tsp. salt
- 2 tbsp. olive oil
- 1 diced medium onion
- 1 tbsp. oregano
- 1 tsp. garlic powder
- 1 tsp. coriander
- ½ tsp. black pepper

Instructions:

1. First, put all the ingredients into a slow cooker and stir to combine. Cook for 8 hours on low heat.

2. Serve and enjoy.

Chili Colorado

It's super-delicious. Enjoy the Chili Colorado.

Servings: 6

Cooking time: 1 hour 50 minutes

Ingredients:

- 3 c. divided vegetable broth
- 2 tbsp. all-purpose flour
- 2 tbsp. cooking oil
- ½ tsp. salt
- 2 lb. sliced beef stew meat
- ¼ tsp. black pepper
- 2 bay leaves
- Red chili sauce

Instructions:

1. Combine seasonings and flour in a shallow dish and add beef cubes before tossing to coat.

2. Next, in your large pot over medium-high heat, heat the cooking oil. Add beef cubes to cook until the pieces are browned on both sides.

3. Add bay leaves, broth and red chili sauce. Stir to ensure the meat is well covered with sauce and then boil.

4. Reduce the heat, cover and allow to simmer for 45 minutes.

5. Uncover the pot and adjust the heat for the beef to cook for 15 more minutes.

6. Set the bay leaves aside and serve.

7. Enjoy.

Cheesy Chorizo Flautas

With the added flavor, you will experience the best.

Servings: 2

Cooking time: 10 minutes

Ingredients:

- 1 c. shredded mozzarella cheese
- 2 tbsp. red salsa
- 1 c. finely chopped cabbage
- 1 finely chopped small onion
- Salt
- Olive oil
- 2 flour tortillas
- Pepper
- 1 c. chorizo

Instructions:

1. In a medium-large bowl, combine seasonings, salsa, cabbage, chorizo, onions and cheese.

2. Put half of the mixture at the center of each tortilla and wrap it together. Seal will toothpicks before setting aside.

3. Next, in your medium skillet over medium heat, heat the oil.

4. Add the already-stuffed tortillas and fry on both sides until crispy and golden brown.

5. Set aside and serve warm.

6. Enjoy.

Sweet Pork Tacos

A quick and easy meal. Enjoy it.

Servings: 6

Cooking time: 15 minutes

Ingredients:

- 2 c. chunked fresh pineapple
- ¼ c. chopped fresh cilantro
- 1 tbsp. olive oil
- 1 c. sliced white onion
- 3 crushed and minced garlic cloves
- 1 lb. sliced pork loin
- 1 tsp. diced jalapeño peppers
- Cotija cheese
- ½ c. thinly sliced radishes
- ¼ c. orange juice
- 1 tsp. ancho chili powder
- Fresh corn tortillas
- 1 tsp. cumin
- 1 c. sliced red cabbage

Instructions:

1. First, in your large skillet over medium heat, heat the olive oil.

2. Add garlic and onions to cook for 3 minutes.

3. Add jalapeno peppers and pork and cook until the pork turns lightly browned.

4. Add cumin, chili powder, orange juice, and pineapple and continue cooking with frequent stirring. Cook for 7 minutes until the pork is cooked through.

5. Put the pork into fresh corn tortillas and add garnish with Cotija cheese, cilantro, radishes and red cabbage.

6. Serve and enjoy.

Chili Lamb Tacos

The recipe is quite different but stands out to be more delicious. Try the Chili Lamb Tacos and enjoy the best.

Servings: 6

Cooking time: 60 minutes

Ingredients:

- 6 halved plum tomatoes
- Tortillas
- 4 tbsp. divided extra-virgin olive oil
- 1 wedged large red onion
- Salt
- 2 tbsp. lime juice
- 12 scallions
- 3-lb. trimmed, boneless leg of lamb
- 1 tsp. Mexican chili powder
- Pepper
- Cooking spray
- 2 stemmed, seeded and quartered Poblano chilies
- 1 tsp. dried oregano
- 1 tbsp. chopped sage
- 1 tbsp. chopped rosemary

Instructions:

1. Mix oregano, lime juice, chili powder, ½ teaspoon pepper, a teaspoon of salt, and 2 tablespoons olive oil in a Ziploc bag.

2. Add the lamb and marinate for 8 hours in a fridge.

3. Remove lamb from Ziploc bag and pat dry over paper towels.

4. Preheat the grill and grease the grate with cooking spray.

5. Season the lamb accordingly.

6. Put the lamb on the grill and add a sage and rosemary topping.

7. Cook for 25 minutes while occasionally turning until the lamb is well cooked. Set aside.

8. Mix the rest of olive oil, tomatoes, seasonings, poblano pepper, onion wedges and scallions in a medium mixing bowl.

9. Grill the veggies for 7 minutes as you turn occasionally.

10. Add the veggies and the lamb into tortillas before serving.

Fish Tacos

It's amazingly fresh and delicious. Try it and enjoy it

Servings: 6

Cooking time: 8 minutes

Ingredients:

- ½ c. sour cream
- 12 warmed corn tortillas
- 2 tbsp. vegetable oil
- 1 lb. sliced cod
- 2 tbsp. lemon juice
- ½ c. mayonnaise
- ¼ c. chopped cilantro
- 4 tbsp. divided taco seasoning mix

Toppings:

- Chopped tomato
- Shredded cabbage
- Lime juice
- Taco sauce

Instructions:

1. Mix mayo, cream, 2 tablespoons of seasoning mix and cilantro in a small mixing bowl.

2. In a separate bowl, mix the rest of seasoning mix, lemon juice, vegetable oil and fish.

3. Put a saucepan over medium heat.

4. Add fish to cook for 6 minutes with occasional stirring.

5. Spoon the mixture into taco shells and drizzle with mayo dressing.

6. Serve with your desired topping and enjoy.

Veracruz Sea Bass

The fish is spiced to give you that delicious touch. Enjoy every beautiful moment of sharing this unique meal.

Servings: 6

Cooking time: 25 minutes

Ingredients:

- 6 canned jalapeño chiles
- ½ c. chopped green olives
- 1 tsp. salt
- 1 tsp. dried oregano
- 4 minced garlic cloves
- ½ c. diced onions
- 2 lb. peeled and finely diced tomatoes
- 2 tbsp. butter
- ½ tsp. freshly ground pepper
- 1 julienned green bell pepper
- 2 bay leaves
- 1 tbsp. olive oil
- ¼ c. capers
- 6 fillets of sea bass

Instructions:

1. In your large saucepan over medium heat, warm the oil. Sauté the onions for 2 minutes and add garlic to cook for 1 more minute to fragrance.

2. Add the tomatoes and stir then adjust the heat to high before bringing the mixture to a boil.

3. Add bell pepper to cook for around to minutes.

4. Add seasonings, oregano and bay leaves.

5. Serve and enjoy.

Mexican Ceviche

The meal is light and refreshing and can be a perfect lunch option for all your family members. Enjoy it!

Servings: 4

Cooking time: 0

Ingredients:

- 1 c. freshly squeezed lime juice
- 1 roughly chopped small bunch cilantro
- 1 diced English cucumber
- 1 lb. diced tomatoes
- Black pepper
- 2 diced green chili peppers
- ½ diced large red onion
- ½ c. diced pineapple
- Sea salt
- 2 lb. sliced marlin

Instructions:

1. First, combine all the ingredients in a shallow dish.

2. Stir to combine and refrigerate for at least one hour.

3. Serve and enjoy.

Seafood Enchiladas

The meal is creamy and delicious and originates from Mexico. It entails a perfect combination of a number of ingredients that are quite essential to your health.

Servings: 6

Cooking time: 30 minutes

Ingredients:

- ¼ lb. peeled, deveined and coarsely chopped shrimp
- 1 c. half-and-half
- ½ lb. fresh crab meat
- ½ tsp. garlic salt
- 1½ tsp. dried parsley
- 8 oz. divided and shredded Colby cheese
- 6 10-inch flour tortillas
- 1 tbsp. butter
- ¼ c. melted butter
- ½ c. sour cream
- 1 chopped onion

Instructions:

1. Preheat the oven to around 3750F.

2. In your large skillet over medium-high heat, cook the onion to softness and set aside before stirring the shrimp, crab and cheese.

3. In a microwave, warm the tortillas for 10 seconds and stuff each with some crab mixture and put into a baking dish.

4. In your medium-sized saucepan over medium heat, add garlic salt, parsley, melted butter, sour cream and half and half. Heat until the sour cream is well mixed in.

5. In the baking pan, evenly pour the sauce over stuffed tortillas and sprinkle with the rest of 4 oz. cheese.

6. Put the baking pan into the oven and bake for 30 minutes.

7. Serve and enjoy.

Spicy Fish Taco Bowls

The meal makes a wonderful option for a perfect lunch.

Servings: 4

Cooking time: 10 minutes

Ingredients:

- Cooked Mexican rice
- 2 cloves minced garlic
- ½ tsp. cayenne pepper
- 4 tilapia filets
- 1 c. fresh sweet corn kernels
- 1 tbsp. cumin
- 1 diced red onion
- 15-oz. black beans
- Fresh cilantro
- 1 diced red pepper
- 1 tbsp. chili powder

Instructions:

1. Combine cayenne pepper, cumin and chili powder in a small mixing bowl. Mix well and brush it into fish fillets.

2. Heat some oil in a large skillet. Then, add garlic to cook to fragrance.

3. To the pan, add the seasoned tilapia fillets and cook for 5 minutes on each side. Transfer from the skillet to the plate.

4. Add some more oil and add beans, pepper, onion and corm to cook until they are cooked through.

5. Then, put a little rice in the bottom of a serving bowl and add a topping of veggie mixture and a piece of the fish.

6. Add a favorite topping before serving.

7. Enjoy.

Spicy Shrimp Quesadillas

The meal is specifically for grown-ups. The Spicy Shrimp Quesadillas is a wonderful meal that will actually be loved by many. Enjoy.

Servings: 8

Cooking time: 10 minutes

Ingredients:

- 2 tbsp. taco seasoning
- 8 medium flour tortillas
- 1 lb. peeled and deveined uncooked medium shrimp
- ½ c. chopped onion
- 2 cloves minced garlic
- 2 c. melted mozzarella cheese
- 1 tbsp. olive oil
- ½ c. chopped bell pepper

Instructions:

1. In your large skillet over medium high heat, heat the olive oil. Add garlic, peppers, onions to cook for 3 minutes.

2. Add the shrimp along with taco seasoning to cook until the shrimp is opaque and well cooked. Put the mixture into a bowl.

3. To the skillet, add tortilla topped with cheese and shrimp mixture then add another tortilla. Cook for 4 minutes on each of the sides until the cheese melts and tortillas become crispy.

4. Next, slice the tortillas into quarters and serve with salsa, guacamole and sour cream.

5. Enjoy.

Shrimp a la Diabla

The shrimp is simply prepared in a unique way so as to give you the best for lunch. Share out with friends and they'll love it most.

Servings: 4

Cooking time: 10 minutes

Ingredients:

- 3 tsp. pickled chipotle
- 1 tsp. honey
- 2 tbsp. tomato paste
- 6 cloves pressed garlic
- Pepper
- 1 tsp. lime zest
- 2 tbsp. extra virgin olive oil
- 1 tsp. white wine vinegar
- Salt
- 1 lb. cocktail shrimp

Instructions:

1. First, combine all the ingredients except the shrimp in a large mixing bowl. Add the shrimp and stir to coat before covering to refrigerate for an hour.

2. Slightly heat olive oil over medium high heat and add in the shrimp to cook for around 5 minutes.

3. Serve with tortillas and enjoy.

Refried Beans

Refried beans can turn out to be among your favorite foods. The meal is easy and quick to prepare, and you are assured of more taste and deliciousness.

Servings: 6

Cooking time: 10 minutes

Ingredients:

- 15 oz. pinto beans
- 1 tsp. cumin
- Juice of ½ lime
- 2 cloves peeled garlic
- 1 tsp. chili powder
- Salt
- 2 tbsp. canola oil

Instructions:

1. In your large skillet over medium high heat, heat the olive oil. Add peeled garlic cloves to cook on each side for around 5 minutes.

2. Next, smash the cloves with the back of a spatula.

3. To the skillet, add seasonings, chili powder, cumin and pinto beans

4. Set the beans aside and mash thoroughly mash them using a potato masher.

5. Squirt lime juice over the top before serving.

6. Enjoy.

Chili Rellenos

The Chili Rellenos is another wonderful Mexican dish you shouldn't afford to miss. With a wonderful combination of ingredients, you will enjoy the sweetness.

Servings: 4

Cooking time: 20 minutes

Ingredients:

- ½ peeled and chopped onion
- 3 c. vegetable oil
- 4 roasted and peeled Poblano peppers
- 3 chopped tomatoes
- 10 oz. shredded Monterey Jack cheese
- 2 chopped garlic cloves

Batter:

- 1 tsp. salt
- 1 c. cornstarch
- 1½ c. cold soda water
- 1 c. all-purpose flour

Instructions:

1. Slice the roasted peppers from top to bottom.

2. Stuff the peppers with cheese and seal with toothpicks.

3. In a blender, add onion, garlic, tomatoes and process to smoothness to prepare the sauce.

4. Combine all the batter ingredients and whisk to smoothness to prepare the batter.

5. Add enough oil to a large pot. Heat the oil to about 3500F over medium high heat.

6. Dip each of the chili into batter. Use the batter to cover the chili letting the excess drip off.

7. Fry each chili for 6 minutes and transfer to a plate covered with paper towel then transfer to a separate plate. Top with some tomato sauce and serve.

Mexican Rice

Rice is the staple food in Mexico. Having a taste of this easy and sweet meal is quite wonderful. Enjoy it.

Servings: 4

Cooking time: 40 minutes

Ingredients

- 15 oz. tomato sauce
- 4-oz. diced green chilies
- 2 c. uncooked long-grain rice
- 1 garlic clove
- ½ chopped medium onion
- 1 tbsp. taco seasoning mix
- 1-quart chicken broth
- 3 tbsp. vegetable oil

Instructions:

1. In your large skillet over medium high heat, add oil and let it get hot.

2. Add rice and stir to cook for 5 minutes with constant stirring.

3. Add taco seasoning and stir to coat rice.

4. Add garlic and onion and stir well.

5. Next, add tomato sauce, chicken broth and chilies, then bring to a boil.

6. Lower the heat, then simmer for 20 minutes.

7. Serve and enjoy.

Quick and Easy Frijoles Charros

The meal is yummy and delicious. Try the quick and easy Frijoles Charros and enjoy it.

Servings: 10

Cooking time: 1 hour

Ingredients:

- ½ tsp. smoked paprika
- ½ chopped yellow onion
- 1 lb. dried pinto beans
- 3 c. water
- ½ tsp. oregano
- ½ tsp. black pepper
- 2 cloves minced garlic
- 2 c. beef broth
- 15 oz. diced tomatoes and green chilies
- ½ bunch chopped fresh cilantro
- 2 tsp. salt
- 1 deseeded and minced jalapeno
- 1 tsp. cumin
- ¾ tsp. chipotle chili powder
- ½ lb. sliced bacon

Instructions:

1. Set the Instant pot on Sauté and add bacon to cook until crispy. Add garlic and onions to cook until onions are translucent.

2. Next, add the rest of the ingredients. Then, cover to cook for 30 minutes on high pressure.

3. Let the pressure release naturally for around 40 minutes.

4. Serve and enjoy.

Poblanos with White Beans

The bean dish is delicious and flavorful but doesn't incorporate many spices in its preparation. Enjoy the quick and easy meal for a perfect lunch!

Servings: 4

Cooking time: 30 minutes

Ingredients:

- Fresh cilantro
- 1 c. Arborio rice
- 1 c. cooked and rinsed cannellini beans
- 1 tsp. cinnamon
- 2 c. roasted and chopped poblano peppers
- 2 tbsp. olive oil
- 1 c. diced tomatillo
- 1 tsp. salt
- 1 c. diced yellow onion
- 3 c. vegetable stock
- 1 tsp. cumin
- ½ c. Cotija cheese

Instructions:

1. In your stockpot over medium heat, heat the olive oil.

2. Add onions and roasted poblanos. Sauté the onions to tenderness.

3. Add salt, cumin, tomatillos and cinnamon to cook for 3 more minutes.

4. Add vegetable stock and rice. Adjust the heat and bring the vegetable stock to a boil for 1 minute.

5. Lower the heat, cover and simmer for 25 minutes.

6. Add beans and toss to combine.

7. Garnish with fresh cilantro and Cotija cheese before serving.

Mexican Street Corn

If you have not tasted the Mexican street corn, then you might be missing a lot. Enjoy every moment that comes with sharing the sweetness of the Mexican street corn.

Servings: 8

Cooking time: 20 minutes

Ingredients:

- ¼ c. chopped fresh cilantro
- ¼ c. butter
- 1 tsp. smoked paprika
- 1 c. crumbled queso fresco
- 2 tsp. lime juice
- 2 tbsp. mayonnaise
- 1 tsp. salt
- 8 ears fresh corn

Instructions:

1. Preheat the top grill of the stove over medium heat.

2. Mix salt, smoked paprika, lime juice, cilantro, quesco fresco, mayonnaise and butter in a bowl and blend well.

3. Lay out 8 aluminum foil pieces that can completely wrap around an ear of corn.

4. Evenly spread an equal amount of butter mixture along the inner two thirds of each foil piece.

5. Put an ear of corn into each and wrap well.

6. Put the corn on the grill and cook for 25 minutes, turning occasionally.

7. Unwrap before serving and enjoy.

Pepperoni Chaffle Pizza

You will love this stylistically prepared pizza. A number of key and essential ingredients are incorporated here to ensure that you enjoy the best.

Servings: 2

Cooking time: 10 minutes

Ingredients:

- 1 tbsp. unsalted butter.
- ¼ tsp. salt and pepper
- 1 c. shredded mozzarella cheese
- 1 tbsp. coconut flour
- ½ tbsp. Italian herbs
- 1 egg
- 1 ½ tbsp. tomato sauce

Instructions:

1. Slice the salami sausage into thin slices and heat the pan over medium heat.

2. Melt the butter on the pan and fry salami sausage for 3 minutes on stove. Remove them and put on a kitchen paper to absorb excess oil.

3. Prepare the chaffle base by adding ½ cup shredded mozzarella cheese, Italian herbs, coconut flour and egg and mix well.

4. Preheat the waffle maker and add ingredients into the waffle machine. Allow to chaffle cook for 3 minutes until it turns to golden brown.

5. Allow the waffle base to cool. Put tomato sauce on top of the salami and top with a ½ cup mozzarella cheese.

6. Put the pizza on a baking tray and insert it into a preheated oven at 3500F.

7. Bake the pizza for about 6 minutes.

8. Serve and enjoy.

Mini Keto Bacon Chaffle Pizza

If you are actually looking for a pizza that will enable you to enjoy the sweetness of a perfect lunch, then the mini Keto Bacon Chaffle Pizza is here for you. Enjoy it

Servings: 2

Cooking time: 15 minutes

Ingredients:

- 2 bacon strips
- 1 tbsp. salted butter.
- 1 tbsp. almond flour
- 1 c. shredded mozzarella cheese
- ½ tbsp. Italian herbs
- 1 egg
- 2 tbsp. tomato sauce

Instructions:

1. In a pan over medium heat, melt unsalted butter and add bacon strips to cook on both sides.

2. Set them on a kitchen paper to absorb excess oil from them. Slice the bacon strips into small pieces.

3. Prepare the chaffle base by adding ½ cup shredded mozzarella cheese, egg, Italian herbs and almond flour in a bowl and whisk them.

4. Preheat the waffle maker and pour the mixture to the center of the machine and cook until the chaffle is golden brown.

5. Allow the chaffle base to cool. Meanwhile, preheat the oven to 3500F.

6. Put the chaffle base on a baking tray and top it with ½ cup mozzarella cheese and bacon.

7. Bake the pizza for 7 minutes before serving.

8. Enjoy.

Pizza Hut Style Chaffle Pizza

Are you looking for a perfect pizza that will suit all your cravings? Then, you have to worry no more. These pizzas will take care of all your needs. Enjoy it.

Servings: 2

Cooking time: 20 minutes

Ingredients:

- ⅓ c. parmesan cheese
- ¼ garlic powder
- 1 c. mozzarella cheese
- ¼ pepper
- ½ c. pork rinds
- 1 ½ tbsp. butter
- 4 eggs
- ¼ tsp. baking powder
- ¼ salt
- 1 c. cheddar cheese

Instructions:

1. In a medium bowl, add a cup of cheddar cheese, 4 eggs, almond powder, a cup of parmesan cheese, baking powder, pepper, salt and Italian seasoning and beat together.

2. Rub a pizza pan with butter and put the mixture at the pans center and spread it to the sides.

3. Preheat the oven to 3500F and add the pizza pan to cook the dough for 20 minutes until golden brown.

4. Set it aside and add the pork rinds topped with mozzarella cheese. Bake for five more minutes.

5. Serve and enjoy.

Japanese Style Chaffle Pizza

From the name, you will definitely realize that a meal taken at lunch does require common ingredients. The Japanese Style Chaffle Pizza is prepared in a unique way that will make your table a perfect place. Enjoy!

Servings: 2

Cooking time: 20 minutes

Ingredients:

- 2 Japanese sausage
- 2 tbsp. tomato sauce
- 1 egg
- ¼ c. mozzarella cheese
- 1 stalk fresh asparagus
- 1 tbsp. kewpie mayo
- 1 tsp. dried seaweed
- ½ c. cheddar cheese

Instructions:

1. Heat the waffle machine to medium heat.

2. In a medium bowl, add ½ cup cheddar cheese and 1 egg. Whisk well and pour the batter to the waffle machine.

3. Slice the asparagus and sausage into thin even slices. Add kewpie mayo and tomato sauce to the chaffle.

4. Add Japanese sausage and asparagus topped with mozzarella cheese.

5. Top with dried seaweed and bake in a preheated oven at 4000F.

6. Serve and enjoy.

BBQ Chicken Chaffle Sandwich

The BBQ chicken is lunch that is worth it. Its tasty nature will leave you yearning for more and more. Enjoy it.

Servings: 3

Cooking time: 10 minutes

Ingredients:

- ¼ tsp. paprika
- ½ sliced tomato
- 2 boneless chicken breast pieces
- Sugar-free BBQ sauce
- ¼ tsp. salt
- ¼ tsp. pepper
- 1-piece coal
- ½ c. cheddar cheese
- 1 egg
- 1 tbsp. lime juice
- ½ tbsp. Italian herbs
- 1 slice cheese
- 2 lettuce slices

Instructions:

1. Slice the boneless chicken pieces into cubes.

2. Marinate the cubes with seasonings, oil, lime juice, paprika and Italian herbs. Mix well and allow the marination set on the chicken for 20 minutes.

3. Melt the butter in a pan and cook the chicken in it.

4. Burn a piece of coal and place it in an aluminum foil using tongs. Put the coal on the chicken before covering the lid.

5. Allow the chicken to cook with a smoky flavor for round 10 minutes.

6. Remove the chicken and set it on a dish.

7. Prepare the chaffle bread by whisking together cheddar cheese and egg. Add some Italian seasoning to add taste.

8. Preheat the waffle maker to medium heat and pour the mixture into the machine.

9. Cook for 5 minutes and repeat the process to obtain another waffle.

10. Put the chicken into the chaffle bread and add a cheese slice, BBQ sauce, lettuce and tomatoes.

Cinnamon Cream Cheese Chaffle

You will definitely need something sweet during your lunch. This does not just come in any way. A taste of cinnamon cream cheese chaffle can be quite a good idea.

Servings: 2

Cooking time: 15 minutes

Ingredients:

- 1 tsp. monk fruit sweetener
- ¼ c. softened cream cheese
- 1 tsp. collagen
- ½ tsp. cinnamon
- ¼ tsp. gluten-free baking powder
- ¼ tsp. salt
- 2 lightly beaten eggs

Instructions:

1. Preheat the waffle maker.

2. Add all the ingredients into a bowl. Then, beat using a hand mixer until well mixed.

3. Spray the waffle maker using a cooking spray.

4. Pour ½ batter in the hot waffle maker to cook 4 minutes. Do the same for the remaining batter.

5. Serve and enjoy.

Mozzarella Peanut Butter Chaffle

The Mozzarella Peanut Butter Chaffle is definitely what you need for a serious food craving. It entails a quick and easy way of preparation. Enjoy it.

Servings: 2

Cooking time: 15 minutes

Ingredients:

- 2 tbsp. Swerve
- 2 tbsp. peanut butter
- 1 lightly beaten egg
- ½ c. shredded mozzarella cheese

Instructions:

1. Preheat the waffle maker.

2. Mix swerve, cheese, egg and peanut butter until well combined.

3. Spray the waffle maker with cooking spray.

4. Pour half batter in the waffle maker and cook for 4 minutes. Repeat the process for the rest of the batter.

5. Serve and enjoy.

Conclusion

The ability to work from home can provide many potential benefits for individuals and for organizations.

For individuals, those potential benefits include; greater opportunities for professional success through improved performance, a better work-life balance and the opportunity to develop and enhance their skill-set in this contemporary way of working.

For organizations, the potential benefits include; increased productivity levels, better defined personal and team performance metrics, improved individual accountability, happy and well-motivated employees, better staff retention levels, and an opportunity for a redefined work culture.

That's if we get it right. The ability to work from home effectively is key in turning this potential into reality.

Try out all the recipes. Good luck!

About the Author

Angel Burns learned to cook when she worked in the local seafood restaurant near her home in Hyannis Port in Massachusetts as a teenager. The head chef took Angel under his wing and taught the young woman the tricks of the trade for cooking seafood. The skills she had learned at a young age helped her get accepted into Boston University's Culinary Program where she also minored in business administration.

Summers off from school meant working at the same restaurant but when Angel's mentor and friend retired as head chef, she took over after graduation and created classic and new dishes that delighted the diners. The restaurant flourished under Angel's culinary creativity and one customer developed more than an appreciation for Angel's food. Several months after taking over the position, the young woman met her future husband at work and they have been inseparable ever since. They still live in Hyannis Port with their two children and a cocker spaniel named Buddy.

Angel Burns turned her passion for cooking and her business acumen into a thriving e-book business. She has authored several successful books on cooking different types of dishes using simple ingredients for novices and experienced chefs alike. She is still head chef in Hyannis Port and says she will probably never leave!

Author's Afterthoughts

With so many books out there to choose from, I want to thank you for choosing this one and taking precious time out of your life to buy and read my work. Readers like you are the reason I take such passion in creating these books.

It is with gratitude and humility that I express how honored I am to become a part of your life and I hope that you take the same pleasure in reading this book as I did in writing it.

Can I ask one small favour? I ask that you write an honest and open review on Amazon of what you thought of the book. This will help other readers make an informed choice on whether to buy this book.

My sincerest thanks,

Angel Burns

If you want to be the first to know about news, new books, events and giveaways, subscribe to my newsletter by clicking the link below

https://angel-burns.gr8.com

or Scan QR-code

Printed in Great Britain
by Amazon